Legends

POETRY BY JOSEPH JEREMY

Tender Reasons (2014)

Confessions Of A Man In His Seventies (2018)

Grateful (2020)

Occasional Bliss (2020)

The Nights, The Days & The Dreams (2021)

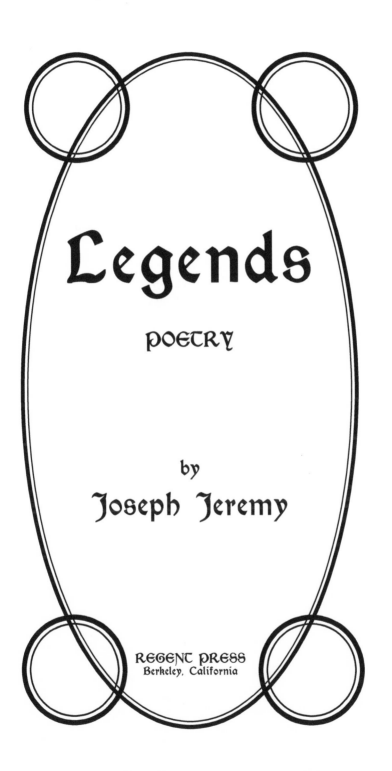

Legends

POETRY

by

Joseph Jeremy

REGENT PRESS
Berkeley, California

ISBN 13: 978-1-58790-606-0
ISBN 10: 1-58790-606-6

Library of Congress Control Number: 2021940922

COVER PHOTO:
Sonoma County by James Garrahan

Manufactured in the U.S.A.

REGENT PRESS
Berkeley, California
www.regentpress.net

That our victory
over every possible negative condition
is not merely possible
but promised to us. (Emmet Fox)

•

If you are putting God first
in you're life
You will not find yourself
laboring
under undue anxiety
about anything.

For where your treasure is
there will be your heart also. (Ibid.)

•

If your thoughts are joyous
Your life will be also.

•

Contents

I.

January 16th, Saturday, 2021

I said
the other evening:

> "I'm in love with you,
> that's what happened
> it explains everything!
> A simple case
> of falling in love."

She wasn't surprised.
My friends complain
my poetry is too redundant.
I repeat myself
so often they're bored.
That's all right.
Let me write it across the sky:

"You're mine, you beautiful thing"!
Not once
but every morning of my life.

January 20th, Wednesday, 2021

I finally
met my match
in 1979.

A girl who loved
passion
as much as I did.

She was living off a
trust,
I was driving a Tom's peanut truck.

We meshed
so well
I stayed for 6 months,
took another six months
to part

and what a six months it was!

What can I say
about a 19 year old goddess
except
she was everything
you want to hold.

If memory serves
we met one afternoon
on campus,
made a date
to go to the beach
the following day.

I remember
just sand and her,
a spring day,
sleeping with her
later that evening . . .

Risking Everything

A little
piano,
A little
love.

Still the pandemic
but fortunately
there's another world —

Beethoven,
A luscious wife,
a dreamer
sitting at his desk
remembering so much!

Dreaming
that he loves growing old,
arising
each morning
living
out his day
kissing
his wife,
walking
the streets
listening
to Beethoven.

Imagining
the finest God possible,
the finest possibilities possible,
following one of those.

Learning
how to love again.

Taking
a chance on life,
risking everything
to live
a meaningful life,
passionately

Not much
just everything.

January 22nd, Friday, 2021

Sun
in between showers,

Beethoven's piano songs, flowing
out of the speaker,

Me at my desk
Healthy, alive, in love.

Father In Heaven
thank you
for my fortune,
my glorious life,
you are my benefactor.
I put my hands
together and pray —
"May I be filled with love and compassion
for ever more."
Asked in Jesus Christ's name Amen.

Beethoven
makes me swoon to his melodies,

to live in the Nineteenth century,
Love
wouldn't change,
would still shine
make everything beautiful.

Yes
I'll take up residence
in the 19th century.

In love with Beethoven's music,
a life
of peace and serenity,
God and Beethoven.

Fare thee well 21st century,
fare thee well pandemic.

Good morning Grace,
love
and
care!

Living With A Princess

Rainy Sunday,

"Don't Ya know
that true love asks for nothing."

(Stevie Wonder)

Gene Harris on piano,
jazz piano.

Saw Gene perform in Oakland one night.

Fell in love
with his renditions.
He lived only a few years after that night,
lovely to see him, hear him.

Always remember his jazz riffs,
he was at the height of his career,
the way he sat
at that piano
like a general with his troops,
his piano keys.

With my sweetheart
sitting in a booth that night
in love with her and Gene's music!
What a night.

Sitting now
dreaming at my desk.
(I almost wrote "Sitting now dreaming
at my piano.")

Glad
living with a princess

kissing
thrilled with the possibilities

King

In the mind
of a king
I inhabit thoughts of you
loving you on our bed,
holding you
close,
kissing
feeling you
move
against me.

Such passion and love
never existed before
I tell myself,
abandoning myself to your love.

Thinking back
I've never
been so happy,
so close.

Your loving spirit
is endless,
just what I crave,
need.

I remain
king
for an afternoon.

A Lifetime To Love

Sunshine after the rain.

Gene Harris
still playing
an organ this time.
Kenny Barrell on guitar,
the tune — *Time After Time* —

"Time after time
I tell myself
that I'm so lucky
to be loving you!
So lucky to be
the one you run to see
in the evening
when the day is through.
So lucky to be loving you."

What can you do
but dream?
Play along
the melody line
until the song is unrecognizable
then come back to the melody.

What could be finer
than living a life?
Not that the blues
won't haunt you occasionally
but what do we have overall?

But a lifetime to love,
A lifetime to love!

A Promise of Joy

At my desk
dreaming of God,

how ever present he is
watching over his children,
us mortals.

I say
"Hey" to you God.
I have great need for you
in my life.

As you probably have guessed
I'm sure by answering
my prayers.

Deeply
in love with you.
Honored by your care
for me and my wife,
keeping us safe
from automobile accidents,
keeping us healthy.

Honored by your compassion,
ingenuity.

The fact that you promote "Joy,"
wonderful.

There are boxing promoters
but a promoter of "Joy"?
I'll sign on anytime.

"Joy" is my aim too.
We are aligned,
joined in a great cause —

to find serenity,
live a joyous life,
full of laughter, love.

II.

There But For The Grace Of God

Rainy
January morning.

Nothing to do
but dream.

(Re-discovered "Joy" in my last poem.)

Raising consciousness to higher levels —

Passion
for the good in everything.
Passion
for the love
that hides
itself in the moment
waiting to happen.

Dreaming of another life
with another beloved.

She taking off her clothes
knowing
the moment has arrived.
Love blossoming,
so many blooms,
never tiring,
always ready for more.
She willing,
there but for the grace of God.

The Match of My Life

Sunshine
for a change.

Middle of winter
a new season to cherish.
If only it would warm up a bit.
Not in winter's character.
Cold is its signature.
(Manage to somehow keep warm!)

Passion,
entangled in her hair,
her lips.

A woman almost seventy.

Regal she is, a princess!

Give her constant massages —

her feet,
her lower back,
her legs,
her shoulders.

To love
it seems to me,
the finest activity
you could engage in.

February 2nd, Tuesday, 2021

There's a point in life
when you have
to risk everything
just to keep life meaningful.

To keep alive,
your life,
your dreams.

Some things are ripe
and need to be plucked.
Others
are just to be savored,
kept
until the right time.

(With Lester Young on tenor in the background.)

Lost
in a dream,
don't wake me.

O well,
if you insist
I'll step down,
begin another dream.

That afternoon
when I can't repeat
what went on
stays with me always.

When she she realized
she was the one who was causing it
she just continued . . .

will be remembered
for a long time.

Start all over
learn to love
slowly and passionately
everything.

Like A Legend You Had Access To

Morning
in the café

Looking across
at her dark eyes
discussing the Russians,
her approach . . .

Her short skirt
on the car seat
looking out the window

wearing no lipstick.

The perfect drive
down the perfect
narrow road.

Tchaikovsky
fading in and out
on the radio.

Long dark red hair
the color of autumn.

Mythological.

Where It Has Been For So Long

In love with everything,
life running smoothly.

I cry out
in faith and love
to you
Father In Heaven
for allowing 77 years
to take place.

I'm not greedy, no
only overwhelming so
greedy for love,
health,
abundance.

You've been so kind.
If I wasn't one of your sons
I wouldn't deserve it
but I am
one of your many children.

Believe my love
for you and your kingdom,
forever grateful,
filled with gratitude.

You are my inspiration,
my personal muse.

The sea and cold weather,
another day to dream,
which dream? Long ago or the present?

I'll opt for the present —

The everyday goddess
I live with,
bow to,

observing her walking through our rooms,
hugging, kissing,
39 years together!
You'd imagine boredom to settle in
but always alive and changing . . .

I pray that it will always be your legend
I'm in love with.
Good chance for it
to keep happening.
It has been so beautiful!

"To Sleep, Ah, Perchance To Dream"

Fortunately
In the Arms
of
many
beautiful women.

To dream again
in their arms,

linger there
for an afternoon,
an evening.

      (You can't forget
      even if you choose to,
      so memorable.)

I remember
her face,
her lips.

Kissing,
lost in her hair,
her eyes,
her mouth.

The chance of an afternoon, an evening,

"To sleep, ah, perchance to dream."

What A Life It Was!

She was 20,
might as well have been 40
for all the wisdom
she possessed.

I stayed for 8 months,
learned more
about making love
with someone
than I've ever learned.

Evening, afternoons,
will always remember
those times with her.

Her body
was anywhere from 40 years old to 14.
I knew so well
as she knew mine.
Like newly weds we were!

From that first drive
out to the beach,
late at night,
to moving in with her
and her roommate . . .
the next day.

What fate
had in store for us
I could have never known.
I was twenty eight.

Now that I look back
her being twenty
had more to do with it
than I realized:

How beautiful it was,
how fleeting!

What Can You Say About a 19 Year Old Goddess?

I remember

when we moved in together,
sharing the same bed,
looking forward
to the evenings now.
Sharing the same dreams
the same sheets,
the same nights.

What memories
live on.
What touches!

No wonder
it took so long to split,
finally separate . . .

An afternoon
in her house in Petaluma,
making up
for time spent apart.

Burning up the afternoon,
only embers left,
embers of our shared love.

She was still 19,
I was in my late thirties.

That afternoon
she drove so far
to be with me.

       Making out
       in the cab of the truck I was driving.
       Finally, we went inside
       laid down.

       Graced
       with her presence.
       Her love.

III.

To Imagine Your Compassion

Where You live?
How love came into your life?

How you reign over everything,
how joyous you are.
To learn from your talents,
your graciousness.
Worth attempting, I think.
"Be Ye therefor perfect, like your Father In Heaven
is perfect."

To imagine your everyday life!
Your love
and compassion.

How much you help those you love,
who love you,
depend on you,
like me!

The Goddess of All Goddesses

The woman I live with,
sleep with,
kiss occasionally,
a trouper, a lovely soul.

I find it phenomenal.
I've lived with her for 39 years,
can't get enough of her,
tried, but somehow
it's never enough.
Always just out of reach,
not that I'm complaining.
In love with a trouper.

Kindness and Love

With kindness
and
love
you can do anything.

Sitting here dreaming
of what's it's going to be like

in a few days,
a few years,
a few seconds.

At this desk, the dream desk
recalling how glorious
it is
to love,
to know
that you're loved.

Her arms encircling you,
her lips caressing your lips.

The Legend It Turned Out To Be

A warm day
in February.

Beethoven's piano.

In love with the afternoon,
the season,
the wife,
the love affair.

A chance to live passionately
the warmth it brings with it,
the memories.

Nothing to do but kiss and hold her
whisper in her ear —

        "I'm still in love with you."

        "As I am with you,"

        she says softly.

No more beautiful words could be spoken in any language.

Just Where I Want To Be

I've got all day
to love,
I think to myself.

Another day
to caress,

fall in love with,

make
unforgettable.

Easy when there's someone you love in the back room.

February 24th, Wednesday, 2021

"I am come that they might have life
and that they might have it more abundantly." (Jesus)

Glorious sunshine
all over.

Spring in mid-winter.
Just what I need!

"What the foundation principal
of the world,
of all the worlds,
is what we call
love
and the happiness of each and all
is in the long run
absolutely certain." (William James)

Like a prophet speaking,
I love positive statements like that:

What I believe — the overall beauty and happiness
of the world, the love, Yes!

"If you understand, things are such as they are.
If you do not understand, things are such as they are."

(Gensha)

February 26th, Friday, 2021

"Here's to life,
and all the joy it brings.

Here's to life,
to dreamers and their dreams.

Here's to life,
Here's to love,
Here's to you."

(Kenny Washington singing *Here's to Life.*)

... Another Friday
In love with what it brings ...

"What the universe
precisely at this moment
as a whole and every one of its parts
is so completely right
as to need no explanation or justification
beyond what it simply is ...
The mind is wonder struck
at the self fitness of things as they are
that it cannot find any word
strong enough to express
the perfection and beauty of the experience ... "

(Alan Watts)

I'd say!

...

Back now from our walk
seated at my dream desk
in love with the sweetheart,
so special.

What I lived for for so long
to reap in my late seventies.
("To the dreamers and their dreams.")

. . .

"Take long mental walks on the path of self confidence."
(Yogananda)

. . .

"If he had not given us freedom to use our will
we could blame Him when we were unhappy.
But he did give us that freedom. It is we who make
of this life what it is."
(Ibid.)

. . .

Well into the afternoon now.

It's Almost Like Being in Love
blaring out of the speaker.
That song always puts me in a trance.!

Another Day Filled With Sunshine

February how could you be so beautiful?
Blue sky.
Yes, an early spring!

The afternoon continues,
sun remains glorious.
Everything you could want in a February,
a warm February,
a new February.
My February,
moving towards spring.

. . .

"You are the master of the moments in your life."

(Yogananda)

Huge responsibility Masterhood,
I'd say.

. . .

Lester Young on tenor saxophone,
tapping my foot,
played with Count Basie for years,
smoothest saxophone I've heard in years.

It's Almost Like Being In Love"
more smooth sounds,
can't help thinking of my woman,
the one who lives with me,
has for years,
my love.

There Will Never Be Another You.
Dreamy rendition,
takes you right near her.

IV.

Sunny and Spring Like

March is going to be beautiful.
I can feel it!

Spring and summer
anticipating warm afternoons, warm evenings.
Concentrating on the woman in my life
elegant she is,
faithful,
fortunate to receive what I longed for.

Universal truth:
Sooner or later you'll run into your dreams
or they'll run into you,

"If
you live
your time will come."

"I say
If
you live
your day
will come."   (Mose Allison)

I'm a believer!

March 2nd, Tuesday, 2021

To love

is the reason we were born.
No other reason.

I find it truer and truer each day.

The lovers own the world,
no question.

Later afternoon, at my dream desk
honored by those last words —
"The lovers own the world."

Received hints
of the truth of that statement
in my teens and twenties.

Only in the last 7 years
did it become a reality.
(Grateful for the revelation.)

Remembering

An afternoon
in her room.

Both of us
standing next
to one another, nude.

What went on that afternoon
I cannot say
only that it was unforgettable.

Both of us
in our teens.
Her mother
somewhere downstairs.
My heart on fire!

She would be in her seventies now
growing old graciously
no doubt.
I wish you the best!

I Say, Isn't Life Exquisite

In love,
staring out the window
to the sea,
on a classic middle of the week,
a Wednesday.

March,
the month of spring happening,
opening the doors to summer.

O yes,
give me the sea and the sun,
A life of appreciation
and love.
Don't forget the woman I adore.
Bring her along,
set her down on the couch
while I paint her portrait.

Love
is best
when
it asks for nothing,
just glows.

Love Yogananda's Passion

"Take long mental walks on the path of self confidence."
(Yogananda)

His devotion to God is stunning.
Born in India,
spent his life spreading the word about God.

I'm such a believer
contagious to read about his devotion.

He concluded his *Where There Is Light* book
with these parting words —

"Those who want to love the lord
and yearn to enter his kingdom
and who sincerely wish in their hearts
to know him
will find him.
He will acknowledge your love
by fulfilling his promise
to you throughout eternity
and you shall know
joy and happiness unending!"

All is light,
All is joy
All is peace,
All is love,
He is all."

Quite a tribute, so like him.
I shall meditate
on my soul and God
loving them both.

March 5th, Friday, 2021

"I have learned
that what you give
is what you get
so give it
all
you got."

                 ("*Here's To Life*")

Love music,
lyrics,
a chance
to live, be alive,
sit at my dream desk.

Cherish being 77
still able to breathe,
walk,
love,
see.

Afternoon now —
sun gone, gray skies
listening to Frank Sinatra croon —

"I know
I never lived before
and my heart
is very sure
no one else
could love you more."

I Fell in Love

with her,
again,
this afternoon.

A matter of loving her
or she loving me
both of them the same thing.

Loving is king.

Why not keep her on a pedestal?
She's deserving
if anyone I've ever known is
it's her,
my love.

Dreaming At My Desk

"Like painted kites
those days and nights they
went flying by.

And guess who sighs his lullabies
to nights that never end,
my fickle friend, the summer wind."

Sinatra's a hero of mine.
Has been
ever since I first heard
him sing a love song.

No one pronounces lyrics
like he does,
swngs
like he does —

"So set 'em up Joe
I got a little story
you ought to know . . ."

"Make it
one for my baby
and one more
for the road,
that long, long road."

V.

What a Singer of Love Songs!

I.
"Fill my heart with song
and let me sing for ever more,
you are all I long for,
worship and adore."

Count Basie and Sinatra on tap —

"More than the simple words I try to say
I only live to love you more each day."

Devoted to love and desire,
his whole life was a love song!
One of my idols.

II.
Night
is almost here.
The dream woman I love
is making dinner
in the kitchen.
A lover she is
something you dream about.

39 years of loving her,
an eternity,
cherish every year, every day,
every hour.

Graced
with her love
for so long,
my fortune,
my life!

What Do You Have
If You Don't Have Love?

Making love
in a dream.
Afterwards,
a dream to remember,
sing about!

I'm not too old
to fall in love
again,
build a life around . . .

Exactly what I've done
built a palace around
our love!
(I can't imagine
being without it . . .)

The Best Days of My Life

Living them, loving them.

What could be better?
An incredible woman,
a view of the sea,
being able to see it, love it!

At my desk
Lost
in a thousand dreams of my life!
Where I was, what I did,
for how long, with who?

Always finding myself
in situations
where I was completely satisfied.
The miracle was
you could actually find them,
those situations
call it luck or great love.
Nevertheless one season
of satisfaction following another . . .

I find myself
in another one
probably
the best of all . . .

My job
is to love,
be overwhelmed with loving!

"Pure and Unconditional Love"

"To develop pure and unconditional love
is the reason we have come to earth."

(Yogananda)

Fortunately
I have someone, a life mate
who is so easy to love.

Developing a "pure and unconditional love"
in her case,
is a treat,
a purely wonderful experience.

Day in, day out.

"Make Life Simple and Be A King"
(Yogananda)

My advisor Yogananda
Kinghood.

I accept your
discretion,
your recommendation.

Kinghood fits into everyday reality
easily —
       Act as if you were a king
       and blessed with a queen.

Not difficult to do
since I have a house
overlooking the sea,
with a woman I idolize,
at a typewriter I love
at a desk full of dreams.

Just to love
is enough
to make you
a king.

March 19th, Friday, 2021

"Start now to think about thoughts that will
bring you health and happiness."

I agree with everything Yogananda suggests.
He is in tune with God.
A mentor born in India.

Afternoon now,
full sun
towards the end of March,
in love with this season,
nothing but spring and summer
to look forward to.
My favorite season.

My favorite woman is near by.
My woman and my favorite seasons,
powerful combination!

Kinghood

Hail to you
spring!

Waited through a long cold winter
for such
a promising season.

Blossoms come alive,
the sun becomes a master.
Everything begins
to relax,
begins loving each other.
Summer can't be far away!

Summer,
the new light alone
fabulous.
Dreamy afternoons, dreamy evenings.

Lying down
next to my lover,
when it's so warm
no need for clothes!
Summer and love.

I'll just dream awhile,
dream away
the afternoon.

77 Springs

The sea
still and magnificent,
not far
just outside the door,

worthy of being worshipped, I think.
Devoured and worshipped.

Almost spring
as it lies there completely visable,
flat and beautiful
just off the porch.

Aftenroon now
spring is occurring,
mild temperatures,
bird sounds,
lovely afternoons,
promises for summer.

Not that I'm immune.
77 springs I've seen.
Always sublime!

And summer,
summer's so beautiful.
I'm not sure it should be mentioned.
Summer takes my breath away!

VI.

More Deeply

I.
Begin the day with *Johnny Be Good*
Chuck Berry.
Fifties happening all over again —
"Go Go, go Johnny go . . . "

Another spring day
sunshine everywhere,
blossoms going wild
What a season!
Makes everything come alive.

II.
Our sheltering from the pandemic
has turned into quite a romance.
Being drawn to each other constantly
has its advantages.
Grown to love her more, simply
to be more in love with her.

Thank you pandemic.
I'm indebted to you!

Love Is Everything

In touch with God now,
make Him a priority
as I do with my woman,
sunshine,
all the great things.

To love the day
the afternoon.

Love is the thing
that helps the most . . .

O
What a thing
love is,
just keeps being.

Calls To You

I.
Count Basie blaring out of the speaker
swingin',
wild,

introducing the afternoon
in a fifties jazz sort of way.

II.
When love calls
there's no walking away
no refusing.

Love is
enchanting,
irresistible.

Calls to you,
softly.

Forlorn

The first hot day
in months,
like a warm revelation

with
my sweetheart
on the last day of March.

Love comes again
to haunt me,
with its sweetness,
its longing.

I wish I wasn't so deeply in love,
though
I could never find an excuse
to leave
she being everything
I've always wanted!

I just wish
I was in a lower key
about it all.

Too intense
be able to relax into it more . . .

Nothing's ideal,
I reason,
nothings perfect.

Perhaps
I could bring myself
down a few notches . . .
approach love from a different perspective.

It's beautiful
that's all I know!

Wallow
in the beauty
I tell myself,
swim in it.

She's A Dream

What I have now I love!

Indescribable love making,
puts me in a trance.

Just put it all in my heart, my dreams,
so I can carry it always with me.

Put me on a balcony
let me sing to her —

Woman
Since you've come into my life
It's been brighter,
fuller,
more alive.

Since
I've gotten to know you
I've
been re-born!

What News — Spring!

April, opening the doors . . .

My life beginning again
with the light.

At my desk
dreaming
of what it will be like
when I hold her again,
what delights await me,
what glory.

What modesty prevails in me
as I sit at my desk and dream.

Warming up again,
try to remember
last spring.
What it brought with it
what newness,
what love
and beginning.

Splendor

Lost in a dream
a dream I won't detail
except to say
I was in heaven
and
she was posing
as an angel.

What wonderful touches
exquisite
full of wonder.

Completely mine
for a day
an afternoon.

Learning To Be More Alive

"But the good goes on forever
unchanged and undimmed by time." (Emmet Fox)

The "good" does go on and on
important to realize
given that much of life
falls under the category of "Good."

Afternoon is here
sunny day in April
middle of April
in a month and a few days
traveling down to Carmel for 4 nights
4 blissful nights.
Time will no doubt move right along to May 23rd,
put it all on "cruise" until then.

Open door,
better for viewing the sea,
feeling the sea air.

Learning to relax more,
be more appreciative.
Realize how great God is!

Enough to be thankful
on this afternoon
in April.

VII.

With My Sweetheart

On a windy
April day, a Sunday.

More in love than ever,
devoted.

When you love
you join God
for he is Love personified.

So eternal,
having a love relationship
with my lover,
endearing,
lovely,
unforgettable.

Why I hooked up with her
in 1982 —
best decision I ever made —
to love her.

Finally marriage in 1986
another perfect decision.

The Will of God

"... and the realization that the will of God far from
involving the loss of any good, could only mean a finer
and better and more splendid life! For the will of God
is that everyone should experience happiness
and joyous success." (Emmet Fox)

Great information!
I would choose God's will
regardless of the circumstances.

Another day in April
to love
and cherish
put
in your dreams.

The light lingers
a little longer now

Right through eight o'clock at night
when it used to be pitch black
now blue sky and clouds
and it's not even the best season yet!
Only spring. "Only."

Seated a few feet away from the love of my life,
watching the Warriors beat the best team in
basketball right now — the Philadelphia 76ers.

Amazing
being part of a couple with her
now for 39 years!
What a love affair!
A real life set in heaven,
living with an angel.

An April Afternoon

"Ask
and it shall be given you;
Seek
and ye shall find;
knock
and it shall be opened to you;

For everyone who asketh receiveth;
and he that seeketh findeth;
and to him that knocks
it shall be opened."   (Jesus)

So positive and glorious that promise is!

Some sun
the sea
in its usual place
just outside the door,
peaceful and God-like,
lovely,
on this miraculous afternoon.

Lester Young playing tenor saxophone
There Will Never Be Another You

There will never be another "her".
How could there be?

They only issue so many angels
every year.